Business English for Technology and Social Media

Execu Speak
DICTIONARY™

Because business is another language.

Translating from ExecuSpeak, the language of business, into something useful and understandable no longer requires a team of attorneys or an advanced degree.

Compiled and edited by
Carol Heiberger

Contributor: Karen L. Jett

www.execuspeakdictionary.com

ExecuSpeak Dictionary[tm]

Business English for Technology and Social Media

English Edition

Lulu Print Edition

ISBN #: 978-1-105-80539-4

www.ExecuSpeakDictionary.com

Cover Design and Logo by Bondepus

ATTENTION: SCHOOLS & BUSINESSES

The ExecuSpeak Dictionary[tm] is available at quantity discounts with bulk purchase for education, business, or sales promotional use. For information, contact Carol Heiberger at carol@execuspeakdictionary.com.

Dedicated to everyone who has been frustrated or confused by American business English.

Business English for Technology and Social Media

About the Author

Carol Heiberger is an independent consultant specializing in business creation. She is an experienced interim executive and project manager of large-scale, multi-location projects. Her industry experience includes positions with the Ford Motor Company, Bell Atlantic, a start-up CATV/ISP, and a large energy utility.

This experience has given her expertise in strategic planning, new business development, marketing, and finance with large complex organizations, small entrepreneurial groups, and domestic and international markets. Carol's approach is simple: she creates effective teams by translating across functions and disciplines with a collaborative and hands-on leadership style.

Carol also has strong affiliations with educational institutions in Philadelphia. She has taught both degree-seeking graduate students and knowledge-seeking adults of all ages and walks of life.

Execuspeak Dictionary was born of Carol's insights gained over her diverse 30-year career. She earned her MBA from Wharton.

About the Contributor

Karen L. Jett, CMA (Certified Management Accountant), of Jett Excellence, works with small business owners who want a strategic advantage to grow their business or practice. She created an innovative Strategic Plan-ting Workshop where, in one day, entrepreneurs create a strategic plan for their business using a process similar to those used by larger organizations.

With over two decades of accounting and business leadership experience, Karen brings a unique business perspective to the table. She understands the operational and financial challenges businesspeople face on a daily basis.

Introduction

The dictionary's website (www.execuspeakdictionary.com) is your source of up to date information concerning books, products, news, programs. Facebook and Twitter allow users to connect, to follow, and to receive a word a day.

Consider purchasing the complete ExecuSpeak Dictionary with over 500 business terms that are defined in plain English and then used in a sentence. In the paper version, there are 18 subject matter indexes plus an alphabetical index to ease navigation.

About pronunciation: The only words for which pronunciation is provided are acronyms that have become words, such as GIGO (pronounced gee-gow). All other acronyms are pronounced letter by letter.

Carol Heiberger

NUMERICS

1337

A written language (also called leet) whose defining characteristic is substitution of symbols and numbers for letters.

Usage: Reading leet requires a bit of imagination at first. 1337 represents the letters leet.

1337 Marketer

Someone who is expert at social media marketing. 1337 is a reference to "leet-speak."

Usage: The staid company was looking for a 1337 marketer to update their web and social media presence.

Usage: Donations to a 501(c)(3) are deductible on federal tax returns.

A

Adware

Computer software designed to insert advertisements into the user's line of vision.

Usage: Pop-up ads on computer screens are one type of adware.

Algorithm

A complex mathematical formula.

Usage: Google uses algorithms combining individual website habits and search terms to present a list of selected sites to a user.

Angel Investor

An individual who provides money, or start-up capital, to help a new business to get started.

Usage: New entrepreneurs dream of finding an angel investor, but it's very difficult.

API

Application Program Interface. Interface that allows software programs to interact. Not to be confused with UPI or AP, which are news organizations.

Usage: Programmers are able to program company specific applications once the API is published.

Application

The actual way that something is used. Frequently refers to computer programs.

Usage: It's not the equipment that matters as much as the applications for using the equipment.

Apps

Small versions of computer applications or programs. While bigger programs or applications may have hundreds of individual functions, apps may have only one function.

Usage: The iPhone has popularized the concept and use of apps.

Astroturfing

A fake grassroots campaign designed to create the impression of legitimate enthusiasm for a product, service, etc. Actual AstroTurf is ground cover that looks like grass and is frequently used in sports arenas.

Usage: People sometimes feel deceived when they discover that the buzz about a new product is the result of astroturfing and not genuine excitement.

B

Bandwidth

Room to maneuver; adequate resources. Refers to the fact that access to the Internet can be slowed if there is not enough bandwidth for high-speed data and large files.

Usage: The team didn't have the bandwidth to take on additional tasks.

Beta Test

The trial run. A term used by techie types to describe the test that makes sure that your equipment, software, and systems actually work as expected.

Usage: The installer ran a beta test before teaching the customer how to use their new home theater.

Black Box

Any computer or electronic equipment whose exact operation is unknown.

Usage: The computer geeks knew exactly what that thing was doing, but to the rest of us it was just a black box.

Bleeding Edge

Technology that is not yet proven and may be unreliable, difficult to use, and challenging to learn. The user may end up figuratively bloodied. More extreme than "leading edge."

Usage: Users of a bleeding edge technology have to be both adventurous and patient.

Blog

An online journal; originally an abbreviation for "web log."

Usage: Writing a blog is a way to increase your visibility on the web.

Boot

To start up electronic equipment so that software and programs ready themselves for use.

Usage: I turned on the computer and let it boot up so I could check my email.

Bounce Rate

On a website, the number of "hits" that come and go; visitors see the site, realize they made a mistake, and leave.

Usage: If the bounce rate is low it means that people are going to the site with purpose.

Brooks' Law

The adage that "Adding manpower to a late software project makes it later."

Usage: If we agree with Brooks' law, then we can't get this project back on track just by hiring additional programmers.

Burn Rate

The amount of cash that a company is spending each month. Typically used with start-up companies that are not yet selling or bringing in revenues.

Usage: Unless we get new investment, our burn rate of $300,000 means we'll be out of money by the end of the quarter.

C

Cause Marketing

Marketing by for-profit companies that team up with non-profits to advertise products and donate money.

Usage: Products featuring a trademarked pink ribbon are an element of cause marketing campaigns to support breast cancer research.

Cloud Computing

Shared services that can be offered via the Internet.

Usage: Companies can replace their hardware and software with cloud computing services.

CMS

Content Management System. A service that manage web content. WordPress and Tumblr are examples of CMS systems designed for bloggers.

Usage: CMS services make it easier for non-programmers to manage and update their websites.

Computer Literacy

The basic skills and understanding of computers and how to use them. Also called digital literacy.

Usage: Computer literacy is as basic to the 21st century as knowing letters and numbers.

Convergence

The coming together of two or more things.

Usage: There appears to be a convergence in the capabilities of cell phones and computers.

Conversion

In marketing, the transition from a prospective customer to an actual customer.

Usage: In social marketing, one measure of conversion is when a browser signs up to be on a mailing list.

CRM

Client Relationship Management. Software that is designed to keep track of customers and their contact information, sales activity, meeting notes, and more.

Usage: The CRM system reminded the salespeople to contact every customer every month.

Crowdsourcing

The practice of using skills, knowledge, and enthusiasm of many people to gather information or wisdom.

Usage: Crowdsourcing can be used to develop ideas for new products.

CSS

Cascading Style Sheet. A type of coding on websites and social media sites that automatically formats content into specific styles.

Usage: The CSS of this site won't let comments be printed in the Palatino font.

Customer Requirements

Features, functions, qualities, and price that have been determined to be important to potential purchasers of a product or service.

Usage: The marketing department was responsible for identifying the customer requirements so the engineers could design a service that would sell.

D

Digital Immigrant

A person who did not grow up in the digital world but had to learn new technology as it became pervasive.

Usage: University faculty are digital immigrants teaching 20-year-old digital natives.

Digital Native

A person who grew up with digital technology.

Usage: Students born in the 1990s are considered digital natives, since they never knew a time without cellular telephones.

Direct Deposit

An electronic deposit from one bank account to another.

Usage: Direct deposit eliminates the need to print a paper check.

E

Early Adopter

A person who is the first to try, purchase, and use new technologies or new products.

Usage: Marketers of new products need to appeal to early adopters.

Earwigging

An old term for eavesdropping that now includes electronic eavesdropping.

Usage: The couple was earwigging the group of teens at the next table.

EHR

Electronic Health Records. Patient information that is kept on computers that records all medical information and allows health care providers to share information.

Usage: The healthcare services industry is making a major effort to move from paper records to EHR.

Emoticon

The arrangement of keyboard symbols to indicate (usually when viewed sideways) an emotion. Examples: a smiling face :) or a wink ;).

Usage: People use emoticons in email messages to provide context about mood or attitude.

F

Fiber

Filaments of glass that are used to transmit digital voice, data, and video signals. An alternative to coaxial (coax) cable, which is made of copper. Systems that use both fiber and coax are Hybrid Fiber Coax (HFC) systems.

Usage: "Fiber to the home" systems compete with cable TV (CATV).

Four 9's

.9999 or 99.99% Describes a level of performance for a technical system that is available for use 99.99% of the time.

Usage: Engineers designed the system to four nines.

Franken-Speak

Convoluted and confusing text that doesn't sound like an actual person wrote it.

Usage: The user instructions were written in Franken-speak.

Freemium

A business strategy that depends on giving away basic services for free and charging for premium services.

Usage: The web entrepreneurs wanted to use the freemium business model.

Freeware

Computer software that is available for free. Opposite of commercial software, which charges for a license to use.

Usage: The student downloaded freeware instead of using, and paying for, Norton's security package.

Futureproof

A technology or strategy that will not become obsolete or outdated in the foreseeable future.

Usage: Fiber is considered to be a futureproof technology because its transmission capacity is limitless.

G

Geotagging

The practice of adding location-based information to tweets or photos so that mobile users can find businesses and photographers can specify the location of a photograph.

Usage: The geotagging program added Google Map info, along with date and time, to the photos.

GPS

Global Positioning System. A system that provides reliable location and time information based on a satellite system.

Usage: GPS systems are used in vehicle navigation systems to provide directions and in cell phones to locate lost hikers.

Guerrilla Marketing

Sales tactics that are less obvious or overt than traditional marketing. Also describes sales tactics that are inexpensive.

Usage: The guerrilla marketing plan included the use of student teams to demonstrate the product to other students.

H

Hackspeak

The language of computer hackers.

Usage: The geeks were talking in hackspeak.

Hashtag

The hashmark symbol in front a topic that allows for Internet search on that specified topic.

Usage: The hashtag #carolheiberger will help you find Twitter messages from the author of the ExecuSpeak Dictionary.

HITECH

Health Information Technology for Economic and Clinical Health. A federal act that requires hospitals and health care organizations to adopt electronic health records (EHR).

Usage: According to HITECH, electronic data security audits will be required on an annual basis.

Hits

The number of people who have viewed a website.

Usage: Some websites have counters to record the number of hits.

I

Intellectual Property

An asset that is based on knowledge or intelligence such as patents, know-how, research, or special knowledge. Abbreviated as IP.

Usage: An attorney who specializes in IP is involved in issues associated with the use of technology, programming, and patents.

Interface

The point of interaction between two computer systems and, more generally, between machines and between people.

Usage: The seasoned employee was asked to serve as the interface between sales and engineering.

Internet Protocol

The popular standard or protocol used to enable packets of data to be transmitted from one computer to another. Abbreviated as IP. Also referred to as TCP/IP (Transmission Control Protocol/Internet Protocol).

Usage: Skype sends voice signals via IP and calls the resulting service voice over IP.

IP Address

The unique address of a computer or other network device on a network.

Usage: The investigator used the criminal's IP address to locate his office.

IT

Information Technology. The general term for the science, the systems, the software, and the variety of hardware associated with computers and computing.

Usage: The IT department is under pressure to make sure the computers are always working.

J

Jock

Someone who is particularly talented and capable on a specific topic. Frequently teamed up with an adjective, as in quant jock, math jock, or computer jock.

Usage: The computer jock had an office filled with gadgets and equipment.

K

Keywords

Keywords are labels or phrases that are used to retrieve information.

Usage: Keywords typed into a Google search result in websites that might be appropriate resources.

Kludge

A solution to a software or hardware problem that is messy, patched, certainly not elegant, but possibly creative.

Usage: The IT guy figured out a kludge to get the equipment up and running for the important meeting.

L

Leading Edge

Technology that is at the forefront of improvements and advances. From a reference to sailing; the leading edge is the portion of the sail that faces the wind.

Usage: As new and smaller equipment is becoming available at a rapid pace, it is difficult to stay on the leading edge.

Leet-Speak

The language of elite computer techies and social media experts.

Usage: When the creators of Facebook talk about their work in a meeting, they might well be speaking in leet-speak.

M

Malware

Software designed with malicious intent.

Usage: Computer viruses are a form of malware.

Mash Up

To combine multiple pieces of technology in a single document; also, the results of such a combination.

Usage: The host mashed up the email invitation by including a MapQuest map, a downloaded picture, a photo, and some text.

Microblog

A series of postings, a blog, with short-form content.

Usage: Twitter is a microblog that limits entries to 140 characters.

Migration Strategy

The plan for moving from one software program to another. May also refer to moving from one system or product to another.

Usage: The team needed a migration strategy to move their customer base from a single product to a family of products.

MMP

Massively Multi Player. A type of online game where the players are connected by a computer network.

Usage: MMP games use high-speed data networks linked to the Internet.

Modem

The computer or electronic equipment that allows information to be transmitted from a computer to the telecommunications transmission link. Short for modulator/demodulator.

Usage: Without a modem of some kind, it is impossible to connect to the Internet.

N

Netiquette

Etiquette or good manners associated with using the Internet.

Usage: It is generally not considered good netiquette to use all capital letters in email.

O

Open Source

Computer software that is not only free but invites improvements from multiple users.

Usage: Unix is the classic open source software system.

Organic Search

A search for products and services on the web that is not driven by advertisements; the opposite of paid search.

Usage: The goal of the web marketers was to increase the number of people who came to their website via organic search.

Outside The Box

Unconventional or creative.

Usage: His ideas were outside the box and quite the topic of discussion.

P

Podcast

An audio program available to download for playback on computers or mobile devices.

Usage: Podcasts are akin to radio shows, except they are on the Internet.

Point Of Sale

The location where the customer is actually paying for the product. Abbreviated as POS.

Usage: A cash register is one type of POS terminal.

Q

QoS

Quality of Service. The measure of a telecommunications or broadband signal's accuracy and timeliness. A technical term, used in contracts.

Usage: QoS is specified in a contract between an Internet Service Provider and the phone company.

R

RFID

Radio Frequency IDentification. A technology that tracks an object's location via an embedded chip or intelligent bar code that emits a signal.

Usage: RFID can track the path of drugs from the factory to the pharmacist to cut down on theft and counterfeiting.

RSS

Really Simple Syndication. Also called feeds, web feeds, or news feeds. Many websites have an RSS widget or button to encourage readers to "follow."

Usage: RSS makes it easier for Internet users to collect content in a central location instead of repeatedly visiting individual websites.

S

SCADA

Supervisory Control And Data Acquisition. A telecommunications and computer-intensive system that manages the operations of an electric utility.

Usage: The SCADA system provides information concerning the operation of the electric utility's infrastructure.

Scalability

The ability to rapidly increase, or decrease, the level of sales, production, or volume.

Usage: It is important to consider scalability when developing a new business.

Scalable

Able to be quickly increased (as in production), expanded (as in capacity), or upgraded (as in capabilities) to meet demand.

Usage: If the technology isn't scalable, there is a risk that there won't be enough product to meet demand.

SEO

Search Engine Optimization. The process of building a website so that it ranks high in search engine results. Search engines include Google, Bing, Yahoo, etc.

Usage: SEO is important because many people never look at the second page of a Google search.

Social Bookmarking

Technology that allows users to search, organize, store, and share links (such as websites or articles) in a central location.

Usage: Delicious is a social bookmarking application.

Social Media

Online technologies that enable individuals to publish, share, and exchange content or ideas.

Usage: Social media are being used to market products and services via the Internet.

Social Networking

Maintaining relationships via an online community.

Usage: Facebook and LinkedIn are examples of websites for social networking.

Spyware

A computer program designed to secretly monitor a user's activities.

Usage: Computer security programs are supposed to prevent spyware from being installed on laptops.

Stats

Statistics. Any collection of quantitative information or data.

Usage: The manager asked for the year-end stats on his performance measures.

Strategic Planning

The act of analyzing the present state and comparing it to a desired future state to create a strategy.

Usage: Most successful businesses do strategic planning at least once a year.

Synergy

The working together of two or more things, companies, processes, ideas, or people to create more than what might be expected.

Usage: Synergy is the intangible quality that makes two plus two equal five.

T

Tag

A keyword added to items such as photos, videos, and blogs. Someone whose name has been used on photos that are online has been "tagged."

Usage: The tags in the ExecuSpeak Dictionary should make it easier to find words relevant to a particular subject.

Technical Assessment

Evaluation of technologies and equipment to determine whether the hardware and software will serve the defined needs.

Usage: The technical assessment should take market needs into consideration to make sure the technology will do what customers want it to do.

Transaction

An agreement between a buyer and a seller for the exchange of goods or services for payment. Also any interaction between a buyer and a seller.

Usage: A transaction could be referring a friend, signing a petition, or making a sale.

Transition

The act or period of time when things are changing from one set of circumstances to another.

Usage: The transition from the use of VCR tapes to the use of DVDs required consumers to purchase new video playback equipment.

U

Undertaking

A subject or task that is large and complex.

Usage: Cleaning up the Gulf oil spill is a huge undertaking.

V

Viral Marketing

Marketing techniques that use social networking to get the word out. When a product "goes viral," many people are talking about it online.

Usage: Viral marketing is not predictable, which makes it a huge challenge to do successfully.

Virtualization

The creation of an unreal, or virtual, version instead of the actual version. Generally refers to the elements of computing such as hardware, software, storage, and networks.

Usage: As a result of virtualization, computing is not limited to things that are in the same place at the same time but rather can take advantage of resources that are in separate places.

Virus

A program that is loaded onto a computer without the user's knowledge and runs against the user's best interests.

Usage: The spam email contained a virus.

W

Web 2.0

The second generation of the World Wide Web.

Usage: Web 2.0 technologies make it easier to create websites without special programming knowledge.

Webinar

A seminar where the attendees are connected to the instructors via the Internet.

Usage: All the webinar attendees were at their home computers.

Widget

Similar to an app in terms of functionality, but very limited in scope such as a weather forecast, a clock, or a real-time Twitter update.

Usage: A widget is a simple way to add content to a website or blog.

Wiki

A web site that allows collaboration and direct editing functionality to anyone with access.

Usage: The students used a Wiki to write their team paper during Spring break when they weren't on campus.

Willingness-To-Pay

The value a buyer places on a product or service. Frequently used to identify the maximum amount of money a customer is willing to spend.

Usage: Looking at competitor pricing is one method of investigating willingness-to-pay.

Word Cloud

A text box with a collection of keywords that helps a user to navigate a website.

*Usage: The big box with words, letters, and categories at the top of the **ExecuSpeak Dictionary** website pags is a word cloud.*

Worm

A type of computer virus that replicates itself to perform malicious actions or use up a computer's internal resources.

Usage: The worm was designed to jam up the computer.

XYZ

Zombie

A computer that has been taken over by another computer, from a distance, usually by a hacker or by someone with a malicious motive.

Usage: My computer has turned into a zombie; it just does things without my knowing about it.

www.execuspeakdictionary.com

Because business *is* another language.

Carol Heiberger MBA   Author, Speaker, Educator

www.execuspeakdictionary.com
215-545-1856